Table of Contents
1. Guest Blogging
2. Creating Shareable Infographics
3. Blog Commenting
4. HARO Outreach
5. Submitting to Free Directories
6. Leveraging Resource Pages
7. Claiming Unlinked Brand Mentions
8. Creating Free Tools or Calculators
9. Hosting Free Webinars
10. Writing Optimized Listicles
11. Building Topic Clusters
12. Using YouTube for Backlinks
13. Optimizing for Featured Snippets
14. Translating Content
15. Syndicating Content on Medium
16. Leveraging Reddit
17. Answering Quora Questions
18. Updating Old Blog Content
19. Creating Expert Roundup Posts
20. Syndicating Content on LinkedIn
21. Creating Evergreen Content
22. Publishing Case Studies
23. Conducting Interviews
24. Offering Free Ebooks
25. Leveraging Online Communities
26. Writing Resource Guides
27. Hosting Free Workshops
28. Leveraging Twitter Threads
29. Partnering with Micro-Influencers
30. Offering Testimonials
31. Creating Seasonal Content
32. Publishing Research or Reports
33. Starting a Referral Program
34. Hosting a Community Forum
35. Hosting Giveaways
36. Creating a Quiz
37. Collaborating with Other Bloggers
38. Writing Tutorials
39. Repurposing Old Content
40. Hosting an AMA (Ask Me Anything)
41. Submitting to Aggregator Sites
42. Participating in Twitter Chats
43. Creating "Best Of" Lists
44. Offering Discounts or Coupons
45. Writing Opinion Pieces
46. Using Social Proof
47. Creating Seasonal Content
48. Publishing Research or Reports
49. Starting a Referral Program
50. Hosting a Community Forum

Introduction

Organic traffic is the lifeblood of any successful website. It's the type of traffic that doesn't require constant advertising budgets, offering an invaluable source of sustainable growth. But achieving this level of organic visibility can feel overwhelming if you don't know where to start.

This book is your roadmap. It breaks down the essential steps you need to take to optimize your site for search engines (SEO) and build high-quality backlinks that drive traffic—all without spending a dime. With 50 actionable strategies, this guide empowers you to take control of your website's growth, even if you're a beginner. By the end, you'll have a robust toolkit to attract visitors, rank higher, and grow your online presence.

Let's get started on your journey to organic traffic success!

Chapter 1: Guest Blogging

Description:
Guest blogging involves writing high-quality articles for other websites in your niche. In exchange, these sites typically allow you to include a backlink to your website, driving referral traffic and boosting your SEO.

Step-by-Step Instructions:
1. **Research Guest Blogging Opportunities**:
   - Use Google search queries like:
     - "Your niche + write for us"
     - "Your niche + guest post guidelines"
     - "Your niche + become a contributor"
   - Example: For a travel blog, search "travel blog + write for us."
   - Use tools like Ahrefs to find websites with high domain authority.
2. **Review Guest Post Guidelines**:
   - Visit the target site and locate their guest post submission page.
   - Read their requirements carefully to understand topics, tone, and formatting preferences.
3. **Pitch Your Ideas**:
   - Email the editor or site owner with 2–3 specific article ideas.
   - Example:
     - Subject Line: "Guest Post Idea: [Topic Title]"
     - Body: Include a brief introduction, your credentials, and why your article will benefit their readers.
4. **Write and Submit High-Quality Content**:
   - Follow the guidelines precisely.
   - Include your backlink naturally within the content or in the author bio.
5. **Promote the Published Article**:
   - Share it on your social media and email lists to maximize exposure.
   - This also encourages the host site to collaborate with you again.

Tools:
- **BuzzSumo**: To find popular blogs.
- **Ahrefs**: To check the authority of potential sites.

Chapter 2: Creating Shareable Infographics

Description:
Infographics simplify complex information into visually appealing designs. They are highly shareable, making them excellent for generating backlinks and referral traffic.

Step-by-Step Instructions:

1. **Choose a Popular Topic**:
   - Research trending topics in your niche using Google Trends, BuzzSumo, or Quora.
   - Example: "Top 10 SEO Tips for Beginners."
2. **Gather Data**:
   - Use reliable sources to compile facts, stats, or tips.
   - Ensure all information is accurate and up-to-date.
3. **Design the Infographic**:
   - Use tools like Canva, Venngage, or Adobe Spark for user-friendly templates.
   - Focus on clean, easy-to-read layouts with bold headers.
4. **Embed Your Website in the Infographic**:
   - Include your logo and website URL at the bottom.
   - Provide an embed code for others to easily share it.
5. **Promote the Infographic**:
   - Share on Pinterest, Instagram, and LinkedIn.
   - Email it to relevant bloggers and influencers, offering it as a free resource they can use (with credit).

Tools:
- **Canva**: Free design software.
- **Piktochart**: Advanced infographic maker.

Chapter 3: Blog Commenting

Description:
Leaving meaningful comments on niche-related blogs can drive traffic and foster relationships.

Step-by-Step Instructions:

1. **Identify Active Blogs**:
   - Search Google for niche blogs (e.g., "best marketing blogs").
   - Use blog directories like Blogarama or AllTop.
2. **Read Recent Posts**:
   - Choose articles that are relevant to your expertise.
   - Avoid commenting on posts older than 3–6 months.
3. **Write Value-Added Comments**:
   - Make thoughtful comments that add value, such as:
     - Sharing a related resource.
     - Expanding on a point made in the article.
   - Example: "Great article! I've also found that optimizing for mobile SEO can boost traffic significantly."
4. **Include Your Website Link**:
   - Add your URL in the designated website field (not the comment body).
5. **Engage Consistently**:
   - Build relationships with blog owners by engaging regularly.

Chapter 4: HARO Outreach

Description:
HARO (Help A Reporter Out) connects journalists with experts. Providing insights to journalists can earn you backlinks from high-authority sites.

Step-by-Step Instructions:

1. **Sign Up for HARO**:
   - Visit HARO (www.helpareporter.com) and create a free account.
   - Select your niche to receive relevant queries.
2. **Respond Quickly**:
   - Monitor your inbox daily.
   - Respond within 1–2 hours for the best chance of selection.
3. **Provide Value in Your Reply**:
   - Include your name, credentials, and expertise.
   - Keep your response concise, with clear and actionable insights.
4. **Follow Up**:
   - If your insight is used, thank the journalist and share the article.

Chapter 5: Submitting to Free Directories

Description:
Submitting your site to high-quality directories can improve SEO and visibility.

Step-by-Step Instructions:

1. **Find Relevant Directories**:
   - Use Google to search for "free directories for [your niche]."
   - Example: For a health site, search "health website directories."
2. **Check Directory Quality**:
   - Avoid spammy directories.
   - Look for directories with high domain authority.
3. **Submit Your Details**:
   - Provide your business name, URL, and a short description with relevant keywords.
4. **Verify Listing**:
   - Confirm your listing via email if required.

Chapter 6: Leveraging Resource Pages

Description:

Resource pages list helpful links or tools. Getting listed can drive backlinks and traffic.

Step-by-Step Instructions:

1. **Find Resource Pages**:
   - Use Google searches like:
     - "Your niche + inurl
     - "
     - "Best [niche] tools"
2. **Contact Site Owners**:
   - Email them with a personalized pitch explaining how your resource adds value.
   - Example: "I noticed your resource page mentions [tool]. My website offers a similar tool that's free to use. Would you consider adding it?"
3. **Follow Up**:
   - If you don't get a response, send a polite follow-up email in a week.

Chapter 7: Claiming Unlinked Brand Mentions

Description:
Unlinked brand mentions are when other sites mention your brand without linking back to you. Claiming these can boost your backlinks.

Step-by-Step Instructions:
1. **Find Mentions**:
    - Use tools like BuzzSumo or Google Alerts to find mentions of your brand.
2. **Reach Out**:
    - Email the author or webmaster, politely requesting a link.
    - Example: "Thank you for mentioning [Brand Name] in your article. Would it be possible to add a link to our site for readers to learn more?"

Chapter 8: Creating Free Tools or Calculators

Description:

Free tools encourage backlinks as people share valuable resources.

Step-by-Step Instructions:

1. **Choose a Useful Tool**:
    - Example: A budget calculator for finance blogs or a keyword density checker for SEO.
2. **Build the Tool**:
    - Use developers or tools like Outgrow for simple tool creation.
3. **Promote It**:
    - Share it via blogs, social media, and email outreach to influencers.

Chapter 9: Hosting Free Webinars

Description:
Webinars can position you as an authority while driving backlinks.

Step-by-Step Instructions:
1. **Choose a Topic**:
   - Example: "Top 10 SEO Tactics for 2024."
2. **Promote the Webinar**:
   - Use Eventbrite, LinkedIn, or niche forums to spread the word.
3. **Post-Event Promotion**:
   - Upload the webinar recording to your site, offering it for free (with backlinks).

Chapter 10: Writing Optimized Listicles

Description:
Listicles are easy-to-read and rank well in search engines.

Step-by-Step Instructions:
1. **Choose a Topic**:
    - Example: "10 Free Tools to Boost Your SEO."
2. **Research and Write**:
    - Include actionable advice and visuals for each item.
3. **Optimize for SEO**:
    - Use keywords in headings and meta descriptions.

Chapter 11: Building Topic Clusters

Description:
Topic clusters organize your content into a network of related articles linked to a central "pillar page." This improves your SEO and user experience.

Step-by-Step Instructions:

1. **Identify Your Core Topic**:
   - Example: For an SEO blog, the core topic could be "SEO Basics."
   - Use keyword research tools like Ahrefs or Ubersuggest to refine.
2. **Create a Pillar Page**:
   - Write a comprehensive guide covering the core topic broadly.
   - Example: "The Ultimate Guide to SEO Basics" (2000–3000 words).
3. **Write Supporting Articles**:
   - Create blog posts on subtopics (e.g., "How to Do Keyword Research," "On-Page SEO Best Practices").
4. **Link Them Together**:
   - Link supporting articles to the pillar page and vice versa.
5. **Promote the Cluster**:
   - Share across social media, email newsletters, and forums to drive traffic.

Chapter 12: Using YouTube for Backlinks

Description:
YouTube videos allow you to include links in video descriptions, driving traffic and SEO value.

Step-by-Step Instructions:

1. **Create Informative Videos**:
    - Focus on evergreen topics related to your niche.
    - Example: A fitness blog could create "5-Minute Morning Workout Routines."
2. **Add Links in Descriptions**:
    - Include links to relevant blog posts or tools in the description section.
    - Example: "Read the full guide here: [Your URL]."
3. **Optimize Your Video**:
    - Use relevant keywords in the title, tags, and description.
4. **Promote Your Video**:
    - Share on social media and embed it in your blog posts.

Chapter 13: Optimizing for Featured Snippets

Description:
Featured snippets are the short answers Google displays at the top of search results. Optimizing for these can dramatically boost your visibility.

Step-by-Step Instructions:

1. **Identify Snippet Opportunities**:
    - Use tools like SEMrush to find keywords where snippets appear.
2. **Format Content for Snippets**:
    - Answer questions concisely in 40–60 words.
    - Use bullet points, tables, or numbered lists for clarity.
3. **Create a Q&A Section**:
    - Add a FAQ or Q&A section to your blog posts.
4. **Monitor Results**:
    - Check Google Search Console to see if your content earns snippets.

Chapter 14: Translating Content

Description:
Translating your content into other languages expands your reach and opens up new backlink opportunities.
Step-by-Step Instructions:
1. **Choose High-Traffic Posts**:
    - Use Google Analytics to identify top-performing content.
2. **Translate the Content**:
    - Use professional translators or tools like Weglot for accuracy.
3. **Publish and Optimize**:
    - Create language-specific URLs (e.g., example.com/fr/ for French).
4. **Promote Internationally**:
    - Share on international social platforms and directories.

Chapter 15: Syndicating Content on Medium

Description:
Syndicating content on platforms like Medium exposes your articles to a new audience while driving backlinks.
Step-by-Step Instructions:
1. **Choose High-Value Articles**:
   - Select blog posts that performed well on your website.
2. **Republish on Medium**:
   - Use Medium's "Import Story" feature to avoid duplicate content issues.
3. **Add Backlinks**:
   - Include links to your site within the article and in your Medium profile.
4. **Engage with Medium Readers**:
   - Respond to comments and promote your post within the Medium community.

Chapter 16: Leveraging Reddit

Description:
Reddit is home to countless niche-specific communities where you can share content and engage with potential visitors.

Step-by-Step Instructions:
1. **Join Relevant Subreddits**:
   - Search for subreddits related to your niche (e.g., r/SEO, r/Fitness).
2. **Engage Before Sharing**:
   - Participate in discussions, upvote posts, and establish credibility.
3. **Share Content Strategically**:
   - Post links only when relevant to discussions.
   - Add value by summarizing your content in the post itself.
4. **Monitor Feedback**:
   - Respond to comments and refine your content based on feedback.

Chapter 17: Answering Quora Questions

Description:
Quora allows you to answer niche-related questions while linking back to your website.

Step-by-Step Instructions:
1. **Search for Questions**:
   - Use Quora's search bar to find questions in your niche.
   - Example: Search "How to improve SEO rankings?"
2. **Write Detailed Answers**:
   - Provide actionable insights and examples.
   - Keep answers concise yet comprehensive (200–300 words).
3. **Include Your Link**:
   - Add your website link where it naturally fits.
   - Example: "For a step-by-step guide, check out [Your Website]."
4. **Engage Regularly**:
   - Answer questions consistently to build a reputation.

Chapter 18: Updating Old Blog Content

Description:
Refreshing old blog posts can significantly improve their SEO performance.

Step-by-Step Instructions:
1. **Identify Underperforming Posts**:
    - Use Google Analytics to find posts with low traffic or high bounce rates.
2. **Update Content**:
    - Add new information, stats, or examples.
    - Replace outdated images or videos.
3. **Optimize for SEO**:
    - Revise meta titles and descriptions.
    - Target new keywords.
4. **Promote the Updated Post**:
    - Share it on social media as "updated" content.

Chapter 19: Creating Expert Roundup Posts

Description:
Roundup posts compile insights from industry experts, attracting backlinks and traffic.

Step-by-Step Instructions:

1. **Choose a Topic**:
   - Example: "What's the #1 SEO Tip for 2024?"
2. **Contact Experts**:
   - Reach out via email or LinkedIn.
   - Example: "We're compiling insights from industry leaders on [topic]. Would you like to contribute?"
3. **Publish and Credit Contributors**:
   - Feature their responses, linking back to their websites.
4. **Notify Participants**:
   - Let experts know when the post goes live, encouraging them to share it.

Chapter 20: Syndicating Content on LinkedIn

Description:
LinkedIn Articles allow you to repurpose your blog content for a professional audience.

Step-by-Step Instructions:
1. **Republish Blog Posts**:
    - Copy high-performing blog posts to LinkedIn Articles.
    - Add a note: "Originally published on [Your Website]."
2. **Include Links**:
    - Link back to your website within the article.
3. **Engage with Readers**:
    - Respond to comments and share the article within LinkedIn groups.

Chapter 21: Creating Evergreen Content

Description:
Evergreen content remains relevant and valuable over time, continuously driving traffic and backlinks.
Step-by-Step Instructions:
1. **Choose Timeless Topics**:
   - Identify topics that won't quickly go out of date.
   - Example: "How to Start a Blog" instead of "Top Blogs of 2023."
2. **Research Thoroughly**:
   - Use keyword tools to find popular, long-tail keywords with steady search volumes.
3. **Write Comprehensive Content**:
   - Cover all aspects of the topic.
   - Example: For "How to Bake Bread," include step-by-step instructions, common mistakes, and tips.
4. **Regularly Update**:
   - Schedule periodic updates to keep content fresh and accurate.
5. **Promote Widely**:
   - Share on social media, forums, and email newsletters to maximize its reach.

Chapter 22: Publishing Case Studies

Description:
Case studies showcase real-world success stories, attracting backlinks and establishing authority.

Step-by-Step Instructions:

1. **Choose a Subject**:
   - Focus on a client, product, or campaign with measurable results.
2. **Gather Data**:
   - Collect statistics, visuals, and testimonials to illustrate success.
3. **Create a Detailed Post**:
   - Include the challenge, solution, and results.
   - Example: "How [Company] Increased Traffic by 200% Using SEO."
4. **Reach Out to Influencers**:
   - Share your case study with bloggers and websites in your niche.
5. **Leverage Outreach**:
   - Ask clients featured in the case study to share it on their channels.

Chapter 23: Conducting Interviews

Description:
Publishing interviews with experts can attract backlinks and social shares from their network.

Step-by-Step Instructions:

1. **Identify Industry Experts**:
   - Choose influencers or thought leaders in your niche.
2. **Prepare Questions**:
   - Focus on trending topics or challenges in your field.
   - Example: "What's your prediction for the future of [Industry]?"
3. **Record and Transcribe**:
   - Conduct the interview via email, phone, or Zoom.
   - Use tools like Otter.ai for transcription.
4. **Publish the Interview**:
   - Add an engaging introduction and format it for readability.
5. **Notify and Promote**:
   - Let the interviewee know when it's live, and encourage them to share it

Chapter 24: Offering Free Ebooks

Description:
Free ebooks are great for lead generation and attracting backlinks when they provide valuable insights.

Step-by-Step Instructions:

1. **Select a Popular Topic**:
    - Focus on a specific problem your audience wants to solve.
    - Example: "The Beginner's Guide to SEO."
2. **Write and Design**:
    - Create a well-structured ebook using tools like Canva or Adobe InDesign.
3. **Host the Ebook**:
    - Upload it to your website with a dedicated landing page.
4. **Promote Widely**:
    - Share the ebook on social media, email newsletters, and relevant forums.
5. **Leverage Backlinks**:
    - Offer the ebook to bloggers or websites as a resource for their audience.

Chapter 25: Leveraging Online Communities

Description:
Active participation in online communities like forums or Facebook groups builds trust and drives traffic.
Step-by-Step Instructions:
1. **Join Relevant Communities**:
    - Search for forums, Slack channels, or Facebook groups in your niche.
2. **Engage Authentically**:
    - Answer questions and share valuable insights before promoting your website.
3. **Share Relevant Content**:
    - Link to your blog posts or tools when they directly address a question or problem.
4. **Follow Community Guidelines**:
    - Avoid spamming or over-promoting.

Chapter 26: Writing Resource Guides

Description:
Resource guides compile valuable tools, tips, or links, attracting traffic and backlinks.

Step-by-Step Instructions:
1. **Choose a Topic**:
   - Example: "The Ultimate Toolkit for Social Media Managers."
2. **Research Tools and Resources**:
   - Include both free and paid options for diversity.
3. **Organize the Guide**:
   - Group tools by category (e.g., analytics, scheduling).
4. **Promote the Guide**:
   - Share it with the featured tools, asking for backlinks or shares.

Chapter 27: Hosting Free Workshops

Description:
Free workshops attract a live audience and backlinks from those sharing or referencing the event.
Step-by-Step Instructions:

1. **Pick a Workshop Topic**:
    - Example: "How to Build an SEO Strategy in 7 Days."
2. **Choose a Platform**:
    - Use Zoom, Google Meet, or WebinarJam for hosting.
3. **Promote the Workshop**:
    - Share on LinkedIn, Eventbrite, and social media.
4. **Record and Share**:
    - Publish the workshop recording on your website or YouTube.
5. **Ask for Feedback**:
    - Collect testimonials to enhance credibility.

Chapter 28: Leveraging Twitter Threads

Description:
Twitter threads are a powerful way to showcase expertise and drive traffic to your website.

Step-by-Step Instructions:
1. **Pick a Thread Topic**:
    - Example: "10 SEO Hacks You Can Apply Today."
2. **Write the Thread**:
    - Break the topic into short tweets with engaging visuals or links.
3. **Link to Your Website**:
    - Include a CTA in the final tweet, such as: "Read the full guide here: [URL]."
4. **Engage with Replies**:
    - Respond to questions and comments to boost visibility.

Chapter 29: Partnering with Micro-Influencers

Description:
Collaborating with micro-influencers (small but highly engaged audiences) can drive backlinks and traffic.

Step-by-Step Instructions:

1. **Identify Influencers**:
   - Search for micro-influencers in your niche on Instagram, Twitter, or YouTube.
2. **Reach Out**:
   - Propose a partnership where they promote your content in exchange for a free product or service.
3. **Track Results**:
   - Use tracking links to measure referral traffic.
4. **Build Long-Term Relationships**:
   - Stay in touch for future collaborations.

Chapter 30: Offering Testimonials

Description:
Providing testimonials to companies or tools you've used can earn you backlinks.

Step-by-Step Instructions:
1. **Find Relevant Tools or Services**:
   - Identify software, courses, or products you use and appreciate.
2. **Write a Genuine Testimonial**:
   - Include specifics about how the product/service helped you.
3. **Offer Your Website Link**:
   - Suggest they link your name to your website in the testimonial.
4. **Follow Up**:
   - Confirm when the testimonial is published and share it on your channels.

Chapter 31: Hosting Giveaways

Description:
Giveaways create excitement and engagement, driving traffic and backlinks when promoted effectively.
Step-by-Step Instructions:
1. **Choose an Enticing Prize**:
    - Ensure the prize is relevant to your niche.
    - Example: A fitness site could offer workout gear or free coaching sessions.
2. **Set Entry Rules**:
    - Example: To enter, participants must share your website or blog post.
3. **Use Giveaway Tools**:
    - Use platforms like Gleam.io or KingSumo to manage entries.
4. **Promote Your Giveaway**:
    - Share on social media, forums, and email newsletters.
    - Partner with influencers to expand reach.
5. **Announce Winners**:
    - Publicly announce winners to build credibility.

Chapter 32: Creating a Quiz

Description:
Interactive quizzes attract visitors and encourage sharing, driving traffic to your website.

Step-by-Step Instructions:

1. **Select a Fun or Educational Topic**:
    - Example: "Which SEO Strategy Suits You Best?"
2. **Use Quiz Tools**:
    - Create your quiz using tools like Typeform, Interact, or Google Forms.
3. **Embed the Quiz**:
    - Publish the quiz on your blog or landing page.
4. **Promote the Quiz**:
    - Share on social media, encouraging users to compare results.
5. **Capture Leads**:
    - Include an optional email signup for quiz results or additional resources.

Chapter 33: Collaborating with Other Bloggers

Description:
Collaborations with bloggers in your niche can expand your reach and generate backlinks.

Step-by-Step Instructions:

1. **Identify Relevant Bloggers**:
   - Search for niche bloggers with engaged audiences.
   - Use tools like BuzzSumo to analyze their influence.
2. **Propose Collaboration Ideas**:
   - Examples: Co-writing blog posts, hosting joint webinars, or cross-promoting content.
3. **Deliver Value**:
   - Ensure the partnership benefits both parties equally.
4. **Promote Collaborations**:
   - Share the joint content on both of your platforms for maximum exposure.

Chapter 34: Writing Tutorials

Description:
Detailed tutorials help users solve specific problems, driving traffic and engagement.

Step-by-Step Instructions:

1. **Choose a Step-by-Step Topic**:
   - Example: "How to Create a WordPress Blog in 10 Minutes."
2. **Break Down the Steps**:
   - Write clear, easy-to-follow instructions with visuals.
3. **Optimize for SEO**:
   - Use keywords like "guide" or "how-to" in your title and meta description.
4. **Promote on Forums and Social Media**:
   - Share your tutorial where users are actively seeking help.

Chapter 35: Repurposing Old Content

Description:
Turning old content into new formats extends its reach and generates additional backlinks.

Step-by-Step Instructions:
1. **Identify High-Performing Content**:
   - Use Google Analytics to find blog posts with high traffic or engagement.
2. **Repurpose into Different Formats**:
   - Examples: Turn a blog post into a video, infographic, or social media carousel.
3. **Share on New Platforms**:
   - Publish on YouTube, Instagram, or LinkedIn to reach new audiences.

Chapter 36: Hosting an AMA (Ask Me Anything)

Description:

An AMA session builds trust, authority, and engagement, while driving traffic to your site.

Step-by-Step Instructions:

1. **Choose a Platform**:
    - Reddit, Instagram Live, or YouTube Live are popular for hosting AMAs.
2. **Promote the AMA**:
    - Announce the session in advance via email, social media, and forums.
3. **Answer Questions Thoughtfully**:
    - Provide detailed, actionable answers with links to relevant blog posts or resources.
4. **Publish Highlights**:
    - Compile the top questions and answers into a blog post for further engagement.

Chapter 37: Submitting to Aggregator Sites

Description:

Aggregator sites collect and organize niche-related content, providing backlinks and traffic.

Step-by-Step Instructions:

1. **Find Relevant Aggregators**:
   - Example: Submit tech-related posts to Hacker News or design content to Designer News.
2. **Submit Your Content**:
   - Follow the submission guidelines and include an engaging title.
3. **Engage with Comments**:
   - Reply to questions or feedback to boost your post's visibility.

Chapter 38: Participating in Twitter Chats

Description:
Twitter chats connect you with niche communities, increasing visibility and driving traffic.

Step-by-Step Instructions:
1. **Find Relevant Chats**:
    - Search for Twitter chats in your niche using hashtags like #MarketingChat or #SEOChat.
2. **Prepare in Advance**:
    - Familiarize yourself with the chat topic and draft insightful responses.
3. **Engage Actively**:
    - Answer questions and share links to your blog posts or resources.
4. **Follow Up**:
    - Connect with participants to build relationships.

Chapter 39: Creating Comparison Posts

Description:
Comparison posts highlight the pros and cons of products or services, attracting searches and backlinks.
Step-by-Step Instructions:

1. **Choose a Topic**:
   - Example: "Google Analytics vs. Matomo: Which Is Better for SEO?"
2. **Research Features**:
   - Compare key features, pricing, and user experiences.
3. **Write and Optimize**:
   - Use keywords like "[Product A] vs. [Product B]" in your title.
4. **Promote the Post**:
   - Share with communities or forums discussing similar topics.

Chapter 40: Offering Free Templates

Description:
Free templates provide value to your audience, encouraging backlinks and shares.

Step-by-Step Instructions:
1. **Identify Useful Templates**:
   - Example: A social media calendar for marketers or a budget planner for finance blogs.
2. **Design the Template**:
   - Use tools like Google Sheets, Excel, or Canva for easy-to-edit formats.
3. **Host on Your Website**:
   - Create a landing page where users can download the template.
4. **Promote Widely**:
   - Share on social media, email newsletters, and niche forums.

Chapter 41: Participating in Podcast Interviews

Description:
Appearing as a guest on podcasts can expand your reach and generate backlinks from podcast websites.
Step-by-Step Instructions:
1. **Find Relevant Podcasts**:
    - Search for podcasts in your niche on platforms like Spotify, Apple Podcasts, or Podchaser.
    - Example: For marketing, look for shows like "Marketing Over Coffee."
2. **Prepare Your Pitch**:
    - Craft a compelling email offering to share your expertise.
    - Include your credentials and a suggested topic.
3. **Engage During the Interview**:
    - Share actionable insights and mention your website naturally.
4. **Request a Backlink**:
    - Ask the host to include a link to your website in the show notes.

Chapter 42: Hosting Twitter Spaces or LinkedIn Live

Description:
Live sessions on Twitter Spaces or LinkedIn Live allow real-time interaction, boosting engagement and traffic.
Step-by-Step Instructions:
1. **Choose a Relevant Topic**:
    - Example: "How to Get Started with SEO for Free."
2. **Schedule the Session**:
    - Announce the event in advance through posts and direct invitations.
3. **Engage with Your Audience**:
    - Answer questions and share actionable tips, including links to your site for further details.
4. **Repurpose Content**:
    - Record the session and share it as a blog post or video.

Chapter 43: Creating "Best Of" Lists

Description:
Curating "Best Of" lists attracts traffic and backlinks as people search for recommendations.

Step-by-Step Instructions:

1. **Choose a Topic**:
   - Example: "Top 10 Free SEO Tools for 2024."
2. **Research and Rank**:
   - Test tools, services, or products to provide honest recommendations.
3. **Write the Listicle**:
   - Include images, features, and unique pros/cons for each item.
4. **Promote to Featured Brands**:
   - Notify the brands or tools you include, encouraging them to share or link to the post.

Chapter 44: Offering Discounts or Coupons

Description:
Promoting exclusive discounts or coupons can attract backlinks from deal websites.

Step-by-Step Instructions:
1. **Create a Discount**:
    - Example: "Get 20% Off Our Online Courses."
2. **Submit to Coupon Sites**:
    - Share your deal on platforms like RetailMeNot, Groupon, or Honey.
3. **Promote the Offer**:
    - Announce the discount via email newsletters and social media.
4. **Leverage Expiry Dates**:
    - Create urgency with time-limited deals.

Chapter 45: Writing Opinion Pieces

Description:
Opinion pieces on industry trends spark discussion and generate backlinks from like-minded readers.

Step-by-Step Instructions:

1. **Pick a Hot Topic**:
   - Example: "Why AI Will Revolutionize Content Creation."
2. **Write a Strong Argument**:
   - Present your opinion with supporting evidence.
3. **Submit to Industry Blogs or Platforms**:
   - Pitch your piece to blogs like Medium or niche publications.
4. **Encourage Engagement**:
   - Ask readers to share their views and link to the article.

Chapter 46: Using Social Proof

Description:
Displaying social proof, such as user reviews or case studies, builds trust and attracts backlinks.

Step-by-Step Instructions:
1. **Collect Testimonials**:
    - Ask satisfied customers for feedback.
2. **Display on Your Website**:
    - Create a dedicated page or section for social proof.
3. **Encourage Sharing**:
    - Notify customers when their testimonials are live, encouraging them to share.
4. **Submit to Review Sites**:
    - Share your reviews on platforms like Trustpilot or G2.

Chapter 47: Creating Seasonal Content

Description:
Seasonal content captures attention during specific times of the year, driving traffic and shares.

Step-by-Step Instructions:

1. **Identify Seasonal Trends**:
   - Use Google Trends to discover seasonal keywords.
2. **Plan Early**:
   - Write and publish content 1–2 months before the season.
   - Example: Publish "Holiday SEO Tips" in October for the December rush.
3. **Optimize for SEO**:
   - Use seasonal keywords in your title, meta description, and headers.
4. **Promote Widely**:
   - Share on social media and email newsletters, highlighting the seasonal relevance.

Chapter 48: Publishing Research or Reports

Description:

Original research or reports establish authority and earn backlinks from those citing your data.

Step-by-Step Instructions:

1. **Choose a Research Topic**:
   - Example: "How Social Media Influences Buying Decisions in 2024."
2. **Gather Data**:
   - Use surveys, polls, or case studies to collect insights.
3. **Create the Report**:
   - Include charts, graphs, and detailed analysis.
4. **Share with Industry Leaders**:
   - Notify bloggers and journalists who might reference your findings.

Chapter 49: Starting a Referral Program

Description:
Referral programs incentivize users to share your website, increasing traffic and backlinks.

Step-by-Step Instructions:
1. **Set Up a Referral System**:
    - Use tools like ReferralCandy or Post Affiliate Pro.
2. **Offer Rewards**:
    - Example: "Get $10 off for every friend you refer."
3. **Promote the Program**:
    - Share on your website, social media, and email campaigns.
4. **Track Performance**:
    - Use analytics tools to monitor referral traffic.

Chapter 50: Hosting a Community Forum

Description:
Creating a niche-specific forum on your site builds engagement and organic traffic.

Step-by-Step Instructions:

1. **Set Up the Forum**:
    - Use plugins like bbPress (WordPress) or platforms like Discourse.
2. **Define Topics**:
    - Create categories related to your niche.
    - Example: For a photography site, use topics like "Camera Reviews" or "Editing Tips."
3. **Promote the Forum**:
    - Invite your audience to join via email and social media.
4. **Engage and Moderate**:
    - Regularly participate in discussions to keep the community active.

Disclaimer

This book was created with the assistance of AI technology to compile, organize, and present information effectively. While every effort has been made to ensure the accuracy and reliability of the content, readers are encouraged to independently verify any advice or strategies before implementation. The author assumes no responsibility for any actions taken based on the information provided in this book.

www.ingramcontent.com/pod-product-compliance
Lightning Source LLC
Chambersburg PA
CBHW070940220526
45469CB00007B/2466